BLACK HERITAGE GAMEBOOK

Keep Score! Have Fun!
Find out how much you already know— and learn lots more!

by Carole Marsh

Editorial Assistant: Jenny Corsey • Graphic Design: Cecil Anderson

Published by

GALLOPADE™
INTERNATIONAL

800-536-2GET
www.gallopade.com

Gallopade is proud to be a member of these educational organizations and associations:

The National School Supply and Equipment Association
The National Council for the Social Studies
Association for Supervision and Curriculum Development
Museum Store Association
Association of Partners for Public Lands

Black Jazz, Pizzazz, & Razzmatazz Books

Our Black Heritage Coloring Book

The Big Book of African American Activities

Black Trivia: The African American Experience A-to-Z!

Celebrating Black Heritage:
20 Days of Activities, Reading, Recipes, Parties, Plays, and More!

Mini Timeline of Awesome African American Achievements and Events

"Let's Quilt Our African American Heritage & Stuff It Topographically!"

The Best Book of Black Biographies

The Color Purple & All That Jazz!: African American Achievements in the Arts

"Out of the Mouths of Slaves": African American Oral History

The Kitchen House: How Yesterday's Black Women Created Today's
Most Popular & Famous American Foods!

Black Business: African American Entrepreneurs & Their Amazing Success!

Other Carole Marsh Books

Meet Shirley Franklin: Mayor of Atlanta!

African American Readers—Many to choose from!

A Word From the Author

Hey Kids,

Whether you know a lot about Black Heritage or not much at all, this *GameBook* will challenge you to learn more! The *Black Heritage Gamebook* encourages students and all of its users to observe the past (history!), watch what's going on now (current events!), and look forward to what will happen (the future!).

The *Black Heritage GameBook* can be used by an individual who can score his or her own points, or it can be used by teams who tally their own joined scores. The book can easily be adapted to suit the needs of your unique circumstances. The main thing is to have fun while learning new information and reinforcing facts already known about Black Heritage!

Carole Marsh

"Tips to Roll Through These Games!"

How to Play with a Group!

If you decide to play with a class or other group, divide the group of people into two teams. Teams can even choose a fun team name! If there is an extra number of players, one may be designated to keep score. Or you can flip a coin to determine which team the odd player will join. Make one copy of the tally sheet for each team or each player. Game pages can also be photocopied for each team or player to have their own set.

Each team plays all games during the same amount of time. When finished, each player or a team representative checks the Answer Key on page 32 to see how many points each player received based on correct answers. Record points on the tally sheet.

How to Play Individually!

If you decide to play as individuals, make a photocopy of the tally sheet and the game pages for each participating player. Each player completes all games during an equally set period of time. When finished, each player checks the Answer Key on page 32 to see how many points were received based on correct answers. Record points on the tally sheet.

To End Play

The team or player who has the most points at the end of the game can earn a reward. Photocopy the reward page to make cards that players can draw to determine their prize. Individual players can congratulate themselves on a job well done!

Be sure to do your very best!

Recommended Resources

Have some of these resources available for each team, if possible, as guides to obtain answers:

An encyclopedia volume or computer disk reference guide

Mini-Timeline of Awesome African American Achievements and Events
by Carole Marsh

Slavery from Africa to the Americas
by Christine Hatt

Black Trivia: The African American Experience A-Z!
by Carole Marsh

Access to official African American web sites,
such as www.naacp.org

World and U.S. maps

African American Reference Library

The Best Book of Black Biographies
by Carole Marsh

1000 Readers Series!
by Carole Marsh

Amazing African American History
by Diane Patrick

Other reference and children's non-fiction books about Black Heritage

Tally Ho! What's Your Score?

Page Number	Activity Name	Your Score
8.	All Aboard to Freedom!	_____
9.	From Virginia… With Love!	_____
10.	Soar Into the Clouds!	_____
11.	What a Wonderful World!	_____
12.	What Makes a Great Teacher?	_____
13.	Black Achievements Through the Years	_____
14.	Word Factory!	_____
15.	Saved Blood Saves Lives!	_____
16.	Greatest Black Pioneer!	_____
17.	Women on the Run!	_____
18.	Speak Up!	_____
19.	Famous Folks!	_____
20.	Halls of Science!	_____
21.	Let's Get Civil!	_____
22.	Black Writers Scavenger Hunt!	_____
23.	Freedom in Florida!	_____
24.	Money Matters!	_____
25.	Spelling Bee Blaze!	_____
26.	Take Me Out to the Ballgame!	_____
27.	Swing Low, Sweet Chariot!	_____
28.	Black Heritage Timeline!	_____

 **Winner!** **TOTAL SCORE** _____

All Aboard To Freedom!

Harriet Tubman helped slaves escape to freedom. The escape route was called the Underground Railroad. There were no trains or tracks, just kind people who risked their live helping others. If they were caught, they could be arrested or even killed!

Harriet made 20 trips, guiding more than 300 people to freedom. If someone threatened to turn back, Harriet would point her gun and warn, "Live North or die here… I never lost a passenger."

The words below are known as an acrostic. Using each letter of HARRIET TUBMAN'S name, write a word that describes her. Do the same for the BLACK HERITAGE side. The first word is done for you. Get creative!

H is for HEROINE

A is for _____ .

R is for _____ .

R is for _____ .

I is for _____ .

E is for _____ .

T is for _____ .

T is for _____ .

U is for _____ .

B is for _____ .

M is for _____ .

A is for _____ .

N is for _____ .

B is for _____ .

L is for _____ .

A is for _____ .

C is for _____ .

K is for _____ .

H is for _____ .

E is for _____ .

R is for _____ .

I is for _____ .

T is for _____ .

A is for _____ .

G is for _____ .

E is for _____ .

Score 1 point for each line you write. C'mon, put on your thinking cap!

WRITE YOUR SCORE INSIDE THE BOX!

From Virginia... With Love!

Arthur Ashe was the first African American player to win the U.S. Open, play in the South African national championships, and win Wimbledon, which is considered the world's most prestigious tennis tournament.

While tennis was important to him, Arthur was also concerned about how blacks were treated and often spoke out about it. He was arrested twice for protesting the treatment of blacks in South Africa and Haiti.

A statue of Arthur Ashe was placed in Richmond, Virginia (his birthplace). It shows him with a book in one hand, a tennis racket in the other, and children at his feet.

1. Which prestigious tennis tournament did Arthur Ashe win?
   a. Wimbledon
   b. Super Bowl
   c. World Cup

2. Tennis was important to Arthur Ashe. He was also concerned about _____.
   a. money
   b. people
   c. fame

3. Arthur Ashe was the first _____ to win the U.S. Open.
   a. Asian American
   b. African American
   c. Native American

4. A statue of Arthur Ashe was placed in _____ to honor him.
   a. South Africa
   b. Haiti
   c. Richmond

WRITE YOUR SCORE INSIDE THE BOX!

Score 1 point for each correct answer.

Soar Into The Clouds!

During World War II, black men left homes in farms, towns, and cities across America to volunteer their service in the United States armed forces. The Tuskegee Airmen were the first black military airmen. Many became pilots, navigators, or bombardiers. Several became officers and many served in supporting ground positions.

The Tuskegee Airmen faced doubt, war, and racial discrimination. Many white Americans thought black men did not have much intelligence, courage, and patriotism. But the black airmen proved them wrong!

Use the Word Wheel of Black Heritage to complete the sentences below. Use each word once.

WORD WHEEL

Tuskegee
black
patriotism
citizens
Airmen
World War II
serve
farms

1. The _____ Airmen were black _____.

2. The Tuskegee _____ volunteered their service to the U.S. armed forces during _____.

3. Some white Americans thought that _____ men lacked _____.

4. Tuskegee Airmen left _____, towns, and cities to _____ their country.

Score 1 point for each word choice placed in the correct blank.

WRITE YOUR SCORE INSIDE THE BOX!

What A Wonderful World!

Louis Armstrong is a legend among jazz musicians. He popularized the song, "What A Wonderful World". Louis came from poverty and rose to be one of the greatest musicians of all time. From New Orleans to Chicago to New York and beyond, Louis Armstrong helped bring jazz music to the world.

After World War II, Louis served as "Ambassador Satch," spreading goodwill for America as he toured around the world. His death on July 6, 1971 was front page news all over the globe. More than 25,000 people filed past his coffin displayed at the New York National Guard Armory.

MUSIC	JAZZ	LOUIS	CHICAGO	BAND	CORNET

```
Z  B  U  G  L  J  C  E
Z  D  V  D  O  M  H  A
A  L  N  F  U  R  I  O
J  A  T  S  I  K  C  G
B  Q  I  P  S  F  A  M
E  C  J  N  D  H  G  T
B  I  T  E  N  R  O  C
```

WRITE YOUR SCORE INSIDE THE BOX!

Score 1 point for each word you find.

What Makes a Great Teacher?

People all over the world remember Booker T. Washington as one of the greatest American teachers. He helped make the Tuskegee Institute (pronounced tusk-E-gee) grow from the first small black college into the large university of today.

Teachers need lots of different kinds of skills to do their job well. Circle the skills that you think would come in handy if you were a teacher. Cross out the traits that good teachers should not have.

BORING

PUBLIC SPEAKING

INTELLIGENCE

PATIENCE

RACIST

COMPUTER ABILITY

GOOD GRAMMAR

SENSE OF HUMOR

GOOD SPELLER

GOOD LISTENER

LEADER

IMPATIENT

PREJUDICED

COMMUNICATIONS SKILLS

RESEARCHER

HONESTY

CREATIVITY

WRITING SKILLS

GRUMPY

Score 1 point for each correct word, and then thank your teacher for all his or her hard work!

WRITE YOUR SCORE INSIDE THE BOX!

Think about these traits and skills. Which ones should students have and not have?

Black Achievements Through the Years!

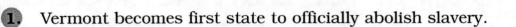

Solve the math problems below to discover some black historical "first" years.

1. Vermont becomes first state to officially abolish slavery.
   6-5 = _____   4+3 = _____   5+2 = _____   9-2 = _____

2. The first black newspaper, *Freedom's Journal*, is published for the public.
   0+1 = _____   8+0 = _____   4-2 = _____   7x1 = _____

3. The NAACP forms to advance interests of black Americans.
   1x1 = _____   3+6 = _____   8x0 = _____   4+5 = _____

4. The "Harlem" Renaissance, a period of great black culture, peaks.
   7-6 = _____   2+7 = _____   6-4 = _____   9-9 = _____

5. Black athlete Jesse Owens sets world record by winning 4 Olympic gold medals in track and field.
   8-7 = _____   8+1 = _____   8-5 = _____   7-1 = _____

6. Dr. Martin Luther King, Jr. delivers "I Have a Dream" speech at Lincoln Memorial during The March on Washington, largest human rights demonstration in U.S. history.
   4-3 = _____   7+2 = _____   2x3 = _____   0+3 = _____

7. First black Supreme Court Justice, Thurgood Marshall, appointed.
   9-8 = _____   8+1 = _____   3x2 = _____   9-2 = _____

8. Black historian Carter Woodson creates Black History Month for annual national celebration and remembrance.
   2-1 = _____   3x3 = _____   4+3 = _____   2x3 = _____

9. President George W. Bush appoints Condoleezza Rice U.S. National Security Advisor.
   4-2 = _____   3x0 = _____   4-4 = _____   10-10 = _____

10. Erroll Brown becomes the first African American admiral in the Coast Guard.
    6-5 = _____   3+6 = _____   2+7 = _____   6+2 = _____

WRITE YOUR SCORE INSIDE THE BOX!

Score 1 point for each correct math answer.

Word Factory!

Make up as many words as you can from the phrase below.

African American Heritage

_____   _____   _____

_____   _____   _____

_____   _____   _____

_____   _____   _____

_____   _____   _____

_____   _____   _____

_____   _____   _____

_____   _____   _____

_____   _____   _____

_____   _____   _____

Score 1 point for each word created. Answers must be actual words – like from the dictionary!

WRITE YOUR SCORE INSIDE THE BOX!

Saved Blood Saves Lives

Everything we do has an effect, or result, on something. A smile usually creates another smile. Even yawns are contagious! This is called cause and effect. Every effect starts with a cause, and every cause creates an effect. African American Charles Drew studied hard to become a doctor and then to become a scientist. Dr. Drew's research on blood plasma changed millions of lives. He became the director of the first American Red Cross Blood Bank.

Match each cause with its effect.

CAUSE

_____ 1. Studies hard in medical school

_____ 2. Two extra years of special training

_____ 3. Works hard as medical teacher

_____ 4. Develops process of preserving blood plasma for later use

_____ 5. Sets up blood donor stations during World War II to treat soldiers with blood plasma

EFFECT

a. Appointed as assistant surgeon

b. Teaches in university medical school

c. American Red Cross models his system for first American Blood Bank

d. Saves thousands of soldiers' lives

e. Graduates with honors

FAST FACT!

The American Red Cross provides half of our nation's supply of blood by working with more than 4 million donors and 3,000 hospitals!

WRITE YOUR SCORE INSIDE THE BOX!

Score 1 point for each correct match. What's your blood type?

Greatest Black Pioneer

America remembers settler Jean Baptiste Pointe Du Sable as its greatest "black pioneer" for establishing a settlement that grew into one of the biggest U.S. cities. Jean was born in Haiti in 1745. His mother was a slave, and his father was a pirate! Jean worked on ships with his father. During a trip to America, a hurricane destroyed his boat. Jean was rescued on the shores of New Orleans. He decided to explore up the Mississippi River and traveled all the way to St. Louis! Jean joined an Indian tribe and even learned an Indian language. He moved to a remote area of prairie (that Indians refused to inhabit!) and built a small settlement with a fort, mill, forge, home, barns, and other buildings. Other people joined his settlement. Jean also worked as a guide for passing missionaries, trappers, hunters, and explorers. Then Jean chose to move on again, this time to Missouri, but his settlement kept growing into a major Midwestern U.S. city!

Use information from the paragraph above to complete the crossword.

1. America calls Jean their greatest black _____ (1-Down).
2. Jean was born in _____ (2-Across).
3. The settlement that Jean founded later became the city of _____ (3-Down).
4. Missionaries and explorers asked Jean to serve as a _____ (4-Across).
5. Jean joined an _____ (5-Across) tribe and even learned to speak their language.
6. After his boat wrecked, Jean was rescued and brought to the shores of _____ (6-Across).

Score 1 point for each correct answer. Just think about it!

WRITE YOUR SCORE INSIDE THE BOX!

Women on the Run!

Many African American women have run circles around their Olympic competition, setting world records and bringing home winner's medals! Four women, in particular, won the hearts of their country with spectacular feats of athletic strength, speed, and skill. Wilma Rudolph, Florence Griffith-Joyner, Jackie Joyner-Kersee, and Marion Jones made America proud!

Can you keep up with these speedy ladies? Write the answers to the questions below. Follow the answers in order to get through the maze and to cross the finish line!

1. Wilma Rudolph weighed only _____ pounds at birth and was not expected to live. Polio prevented her from walking for years, but she later ran track.

2. Wilma won 3 gold _____ in the 1960 Olympics and was named Female Athlete of the Year!

3. Marion Jones played many _____ while growing up, and even studied gymnastics and ballet!

4. Marion won 5 medals in track and field in the 2000 Olympics. She set a world _____ for the number of medals won in a single Olympics!

5. Florence Griffith-Joyner won 1 _____ medal at her first Olympics in 1984. She later won 3 gold medals and 1 silver medal in the 1988 Olympics.

6. Florence's fans called her Flojo. She married another _____!

7. Jackie Joyner-Kersee ran in four different Olympic Games. She won 3 gold medals, 1 silver, and 1 bronze during her Olympic _____.

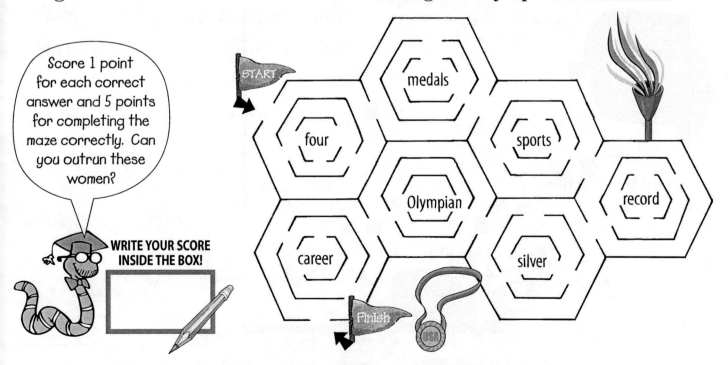

Score 1 point for each correct answer and 5 points for completing the maze correctly. Can you outrun these women?

WRITE YOUR SCORE INSIDE THE BOX!

START

medals

four

sports

Olympian

record

career

silver

Finish

Speak Up!

Many white Southerners assumed that their black slaves weren't very smart. Black slaves were not allowed to learn how to read and write. However, some blacks were educated by their masters to increase usefulness. Many free or escaped blacks learned to read and write on their own. Some even became skilled orators, or public speakers, like Frederick Douglass and Sojourner Truth. These leaders used their skills to inspire change. Today reading and writing are skills that all African Americans can obtain. Many use their skills, like Frederick and Sojourner, to become public speakers who speak out for change in our society.

Read the two lists of facts about each black orator. Circle each fact that Frederick and Sojourner have in common. Remember the phrase doesn't have to be exactly the same, but the idea must be similar.

Frederick Douglass	Sojourner Truth
abolitionist	born into slavery
learned to read	freed by New York Law
worked in a shipyard	changed name from Isabella Baumfree
became Minister to Haiti	name means "traveler for truth"
asked President Lincoln to free slaves	preacher woman
born into slavery	helped escaped slaves find jobs
runaway slave	abolitionist
served in government	could read and write
bought own freedom	advises President Lincoln about slaves
African American hero	African American hero
published black newspaper	skilled religious orator
skilled political orator	spoke for women's rights
active in Underground Railroad	first black woman to speak against slavery

Score 1 point for each correct match. Speak out! (but not when your teacher is talking!)

WRITE YOUR SCORE INSIDE THE BOX!

Famous Folk!

There are some famous folks in the world about whom everyone should know something. Do you recognize all these names and accomplishments?

Put the initials of each person in front of their fact.

Initials

(blank rounded boxes for each fact)

Fact

Minister who had a dream about equality and told the nation

Helped the Chicago Bulls basketball team win 5 NBA Championships

Refused to give up her bus seat in Montgomery, Alabama

Won a Pulitzer Prize for writing the novel *Beloved*

General who served in the Persian Gulf War

First black female mayor of a major U.S. city (Atlanta)

Escaped slavery and then established the Underground Railroad

Names

Shirley Franklin, *city manager*

Harriet Tubman, *fugitive*

Martin Luther King, Jr., *civil rights orator*

Rosa Parks, *bus rider*

Michael Jordan, *dribbler*

Toni Morrison, *author*

Colin Powell, *general*

Score 1 point for each correct match.

WRITE YOUR SCORE INSIDE THE BOX!

Halls of Science!

African American scientists help make American lives better.

- The research of Dr. Ernest Just led to further knowledge of the biology of cells.
- Dr. Jane Wright is known in her field for expert cancer research.
- Chemist Percy Julian developed more affordable drugs to treat arthritis and an eye disease
- Dr. Charles Drew researched a way to preserve blood plasma.

Help each scientist find his or her way home. Color the houses! Write the correct person's initials on each door.

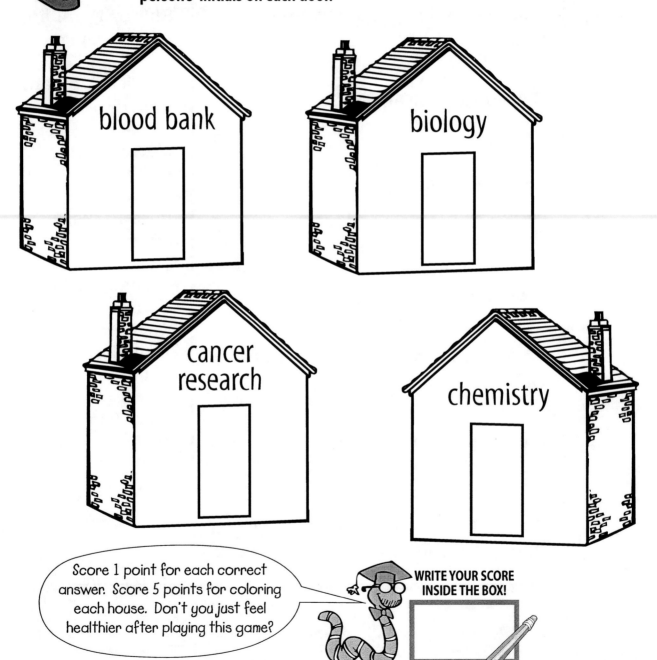

blood bank

biology

cancer research

chemistry

Score 1 point for each correct answer. Score 5 points for coloring each house. Don't you just feel healthier after playing this game?

WRITE YOUR SCORE INSIDE THE BOX!

Let's get Civil!

African Americans were not treated equally after the Emancipation Proclamation set them free. Blacks could not enjoy the same rights, privileges, or freedoms as the rest of America for many years. Blacks couldn't vote, own weapons, run for political office, or even work certain jobs. Schools, restaurants, neighborhoods, churches, even drinking fountains were all separate for black and white citizens.

Dr. Martin Luther King, Jr., a black minister, tried to end the separation by working hard for equal rights. He spoke for blacks, but wanted people of all skin colors to get along. He encouraged civil disobedience, or peaceful protesting without violence. Other civil rights heroes (such as Rosa Parks, W.E.B. Du Bois, and Thurgood Marshall) also helped bring about lasting change for African Americans.

Crack the code to write words that are associated with the Civil Rights Movement.

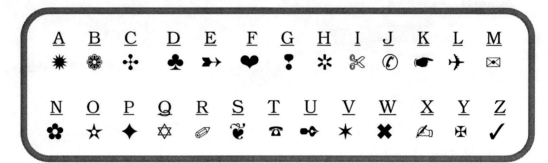

1. ___ ___ ___ ___ ___ ___

2. ___ ___ ___ ___ ___

3. ___ ___ ___ ___ ___

4. ___ ___ ___ ___ ___ ___

5. ___ ___ ___ ___ ___ ___ ___ ___ ___

6. ___ ___ ___ ___ ___ ___

7. ___ ___ ___ ___ ___

8. ___ ___ ___ ___ ___ ___ ___ ___

9. ___ ___ ___ ___ ___ ___ ___ ___

10. ___ ___ ___ ___ ___ ___

WRITE YOUR SCORE INSIDE THE BOX!

Score 1 point for each correct answer. Put on your detective hats!

Black Writers Scavenger Hunt!

Many black writers have given the world new ideas, thoughts, and theories about life. They serve as an important part of American culture.

Read the list of black writers below. You might not recognize them all! Go on a scavenger hunt and research one title (book, poem, etc...) for each writer. Use an encyclopedia, almanac, library book, the Internet, or even an expert!

> Poetry from *The Weary Blues*
>
> We cry among the skyscrapers
> As our ancestors
> Cried among the palms of Africa
> Because we are alone,
> It is night,
> And we're afraid.
>
> **Langston Hughes**

WRITER	TITLE
1. Toni Morrison	_____
2. Maya Angelou	_____
3. Paul Lawrence Dunbar	_____
4. Langston Hughes	_____
5. Alice Walker	_____
6. Toni Cade Bambara	_____
7. Gwendolyn Brooks	_____
8. W.E.B. Du Bois	_____
9. Phillis Wheatley	_____
10. Rita Dove	_____
11. Countee Cullen	_____
12. Eldridge Cleaver	_____
13. Frederick Douglas	_____
14. Booker T. Washington	_____
15. Claude McKay	_____

Score 1 point for a valid title researched for each person. Only 1 title each!

WRITE YOUR SCORE INSIDE THE BOX!

Freedom in Florida!

Did you know that free blacks lived in Florida during the 1600 and 1700s? Spain controlled Florida during that time, while Great Britain controlled... well, most everything else! The Spaniards set up a community called Fort Mose for escaped black slaves. All were welcome as long as they become Catholics. Nearly 100 black men, women, and children lived at Fort Mose. The black families farmed the surrounding lands for their living. Then the British tried to make Spain leave America for good. They attacked and destroyed Fort Mose. Black soldiers helped the Spaniards save the St. Augustine settlement. The blacks fought hard because they knew that their freedom would be lost if the British won. The British were beaten (for the time being) and St. Augustine was saved!

Help the escaping slave girl and her family find the settlement of St. Augustine before the British find it!

START

FINISH ▶

WRITE YOUR SCORE INSIDE THE BOX!

Score 5 points for correctly finding your way through the maze. Don't get lost!

$$Money Matters!$$

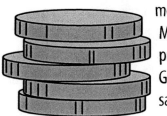

How much money do you have saved up at home right now? How do you earn money? Do you do chores at home for an allowance, mow lawns, baby-sit, walk dogs, help clean houses, sell lemonade? All these ways to earn money are great. It is important to know how much money to spend and how much to save. Maggie Lena Walker sure knew when to save money. She was the first female bank president in 1903. Maggie headed the St. Luke Penny Savings Bank. It was founded by the Grand United Order of St. Luke, a group of people who taught African Americans how to save money and support each other in business.

Add the coins together and write the correct dollar amount in the blank.

1. 1 dime, 3 nickels, 1 quarter _____

2. 4 quarters, 3 pennies, 1 half-dollar _____

3. 6 dimes, 6 nickels, 6 pennies _____

4. 7 pennies, 1 quarter, 2 nickels _____

5. 5 nickels, 8 dimes, 3 quarters _____

6. 2 half-dollars, 2 quarters _____

7. 3 dimes, 6 pennies, 2 nickels _____

8. 6 quarters, 3 dimes, 4 nickels _____

9. 1 quarter, 1 dime, 1 nickel, 1 penny _____

10. 3 quarters, 4 nickels, 8 pennies, 2 dimes _____

Score 1 point for each amount added correctly. Don't spend all your points in one place!

WRITE YOUR SCORE INSIDE THE BOX!

Spelling Bee Blaze!

Help! A fire is spreading to the library, and the adults are too busy preparing for the African American Spelling Bee to notice! Correct the misspelled words below, and tell someone to call 911!

WORD	CORRECT SPELLING
freeedoom	_____
Africaan	_____
haritage	_____
sivil ritghes	_____
diskrimation	_____
slavry	_____
Undagrund Railrood	_____
hisktory	_____
sejregation	_____
boiiicot	_____

WRITE YOUR SCORE INSIDE THE BOX!

Score 1 point for each correct spelled word. Wacth yur spelinng noww!

Sprint, Shoot, Strike, Swing, Score!

African American athletes participate in many sports. Black athletes were often not allowed to compete with white athletes, but laws and traditions changed.

Blacks were not allowed to play in the major baseball leagues. Then Jackie Robinson signed with the Brooklyn Dodgers in 1947. Walter Payton, who played for the Chicago Bears, is known as one of the greatest running backs of all time. He paved the way for black football greats like O.J. Simpson, Emmit Smith, and Michael Irving.

Tiger Woods, a young black golf star, broken several records. In 2002, he became the youngest golfer to win eight PGA major titles! African American Joe Louis (a.k.a. "The Brown Bomber") became the world heavyweight champion, and the first boxer to hold that title for longer than a decade.

Basketball is a favorite sport among African American athletes. Star such as Michael Jordan, Wilt Chamberlain, Kareem Abdul-Jabbar, Sheryl Swoopes, Patrick Ewing, and David Robinson helped create a new fans for basketball.

The contributions of black athletes over the decades has increased the popularity of sports in America.

Unscramble the words to complete the sentences about African American sports heroes.

1. Joe Louis was nicknamed the (WBRNO) (BMREOB)
   _____ _____ in boxing.

2. Black baseball players competed in the (GROEN LLSEBABA)
   _____ _____ League.

3. (LWTRAE) (YTNPAO) _____ _____ played for the
   Chicago Bears.

4. Tiger Woods won (GEHTI) _____ major PGA titles in golf.

5. Jackie Robinson broke the color (BRRREIA) _____ in baseball

Score 1 point for each correctly unscrambled word. Get swinging and get running!

WRITE YOUR SCORE
INSIDE THE BOX!

Swing Low, Sweet Chariot!

Many African American slaves sang spirituals, or religious songs. Blacks sang spirituals for many different reasons. These songs could worship God, celebrate joy, express sorrow and pain, and even communicate secret messages, . Most black spirituals are about trial, sorrow, and the hope for freedom. Today many of the beautiful spirituals that were preserved are still sung, performed, and recorded for public enjoyment!

"A keen observer might have detected in our repeated singing of 'O Canaan, sweet Canaan, I am bound for the land of Canaan' something more than a hope of reaching heaven."
– Frederick Douglass

"When dat ar ole chariot comes,
I'm gwine to lebe you,
I'm boun' for de promised land,
Frien's, I'm gwine to lebe you."

"I'm sorry, frien's, to lebe you,
Farewell! oh, farewell!
But I'll meet you in de mornin',
Farewell! oh, farewell!
"I'll meet you in de mornin',
When you reach de promised land;
On de oder side of Jordan,
For I'm boun' for de promised land."

How many lines are in the song?   _____
How many adjectives are used?   _____
How many nouns are used?   _____
How many stanzas are listed?   _____
How many single verbs are used?   _____
How many contractions are used?   _____
How many pronouns are used?   _____

Find antonyms (opposites) for the following words.

farewell _____   morning _____   come _____
leave _____   friend _____

What secret message does the song communicate? _____

_____

WRITE YOUR SCORE INSIDE THE BOX!

Score 1 point for each correct answer. Score another 5 points if you can sing the song for your class!

Black History Timeline

A timeline is a list of important events and the year that they happened. You can use a timeline to understand more about history.

Read this mixed up timeline about black history. Number the 15 events in chronological order.

DATE   **EVENT**

____ 1963   Dr. Martin Luther King, Jr. delivers "I Have a Dream" speech.

____ 1937   Black boxer Joe Louis becomes world heavyweight champion.

____ 1863   Lincoln issues Emancipation Proclamation, frees U.S. slaves.

____ 1976   Black historian Carter G. Woodson creates Black History Month.

____ 1770   Crispus Attacks becomes first casualty of the American Revolution.

____ 1758   African Baptist Church, first known black church, is established.

____ 1865   Thirteenth constitutional amendment abolishes U.S. slavery.

____ 1942   Black "Tuskegee Airmen" fly in World War II combat missions.

____ 1950   U.S. Supreme Court declares school segregation unconstitutional.

____ 1827   *Freedom's Journal*, first black newspaper published.

____ 1965   Voting Rights Acts allows blacks to vote freely.

____ 1909   NAACP formed to advance interests of colored people.

____ 1967   First black Supreme Court Justice, Thurgood Marshall, appointed.

Score 1 point for each correctly numbered event. Don't get lost in time!

WRITE YOUR SCORE INSIDE THE BOX!

Score Results!

Congratulations! You did it! Now that you've completed your GameBook, let's see how well you did. Be sure to use the tally sheet on page 7 to add up all your points. Once you get your FINAL score, write it in the box below! Then use the point ranges to see what your score means.

FINAL SCORE

221 & up	**YOU COULD WRITE THIS BOOK YOURSELF!!!**
201 - 220	**YOU'RE A GENIUS!!!**
181 - 200	**SUPERSMART ALERT!!!**
151 - 180	**WATCH OUT - SMART KID ON THE RUN!!!**
121 - 150	**WOW! YOU LEARNED A WHOLE LOT!!!**
0 - 120	**TRY HARDER - YOU CAN DO IT!!!**

Excellent! You did an awesome job!

REWARDS! REWARDS! REWARDS!

Be sure to photocopy this page!

Here's A Quarter!

This card entitles holder to a quarter!

FIRST IN LINE CARD!

This card entitles holder to be first in line for one day!

A Round Of Applause From The Class!

This pass entitles holder to receive applause from classmates!

EXTRA LIBRARY TIME!

This card entitles holder to extra library time!

Homework Tonight!

This card entitles holder to skip their homework for one night!

Go to Lunch First!

This pass entitles holder to be first in line for lunch!

Sing In Class!

This card entitles the holder to sing aloud in class!

Share Your Knowledge!

This pass entitles holder to visit another class and share something we've learned!

Extra Recess Time!

This pass entitles holder to extra recess time!

Free Hall Pass!

This card gives you free pass today!

Smile & Bow!

You did it! Take a minute to smile and bow for us!

Make Us A Question!

This card entitles holder to make up a question!

Special Treat Card!

This pass entitles holder to one special treat!

Be The Teacher's Pet!

This card entitles holder to be the teachers pet!

Stand & Stretch!

This card entitles holder to stand and stretch for a minute!

I Owe You Candy!

This pass entitles the holder to some yummy candy!

Official

BLACK HERITAGE GAMEBOOK

Certificate

Presented to:

_____

This certificate verifies that the above named
is officially an intellectual of The African American Experience!

_____
Signature

_____
Date

Answer Key

Page 8 — Variable – check with teacher.

Page 9 — 1-A; 2-B; 3-B; 4-B

Page 10 — Tuskegee, citizens, World War II, black, patriotism, farms, serve

Page 11

```
Z  B  U  G  L  J  C  E
Z  D  V  D  O  M  H  A
A  L  N  F  U  R  I  O
J  A  T  S  I  K  C  G
B  Q  I  P  S  F  A  M
E  C  J  N  D  H  G  T
B  I  T  E  N  R  O  C
```

Page 12 — Circle: leader, intelligence, patience, good listener, honesty, creativity, sense of humor, public speaking, computer ability, researcher, good math skills, writer, communication skills, good speller, good grammar
Cross Out: grumpy, impatient, boring, racist

Page 13 — 1–1777; 2–1827; 3–1909; 4–1920; 5–1936; 6–1963; 7–1967; 8–1976; 9–2000; 10–1998

Page 14 — Variable – check with teacher.

Page 15 — 1-e; 2-b; 3-a; 4-c; 5-d

Page 16 — 1-pioneer; 2-Haiti; 3-Chicago; 4-guide; 5-Indian; 6-New Orleans

Page 17 — 1-four; 2-medals; 3-sports; 4-record; 5-silver; 6-Olympian; 7-career

Page 18 — Similarities: abolitionist, skilled orator, born into slavery, advised President Lincoln, could read, African American hero

Page 19 — MK, MJ, RP, TM, CP, SF, BH, HT, LH

Page 20 — Dr. Percy Julian (chemistry), Dr. Jane Wright (cancer research), Dr. Charles Drew (blood bank), Dr. Ernest Just (biology)

Page 21 — 1-racism; 2-equal; 3-voter; 4-rights; 5-prejudice; 6-change; 7-peace; 8-freedoms; 9-separate; 10-heroes

Page 22 — Variable – check with teacher.

Page 23 — Variable – check with teacher.

Page 24 — 1-$0.50; 2-$1.53; 3-$0.96; 4-$0.42; 5-$1.80; 6-$1.50; 7-$0.46; 8-$2.00; 9-$0.41; 10-$1.23

Page 25 — freedom, African, heritage, civil rights, discrimination, slavery, Underground Railroad, history, segregation, boycott

Page 26 — 1. Brown Bomber; 2. Negro Baseball; 3. Walter Payton; 4. eight; 5. barrier

Page 27 — 12, 5, 10, 2, 9, 7, 13
hello, evening, go, stay, enemy (or similar)
The song communicates a plan to escape towards freedom.

Page 28 — 10, 7, 4, 13, 2, 1, 5, 8, 9, 3, 11, 6, 12